The
Flappy Parts

Kevin L. Donihe's Books

Kevin L. Donihe

The Flappy Parts

A Lazy Fascist Paperbook

Some of these poems first appeared in Bathtub Gin, Black Petals, Bust Down the Door and Eat All the Chickens, Book of Dark Wisdom, Café Irreal, ChiZine, The Dream People, Dreams and Nightmares, Electric Velocipede, First Base Publishing, Flesh and Blood, Frisson, Hadrosaur Tales Magazine, Horror Carousel, Idiot's Manifesto, Kitty Litter Press, Lethologica, Liquid Ohio, Lullaby Hearse, Lunatic Chameleon, Macabre, The Magazine of Bizarro Fiction, Mausoleum, Mouseion, My Favorite Bullet, NFG, Not One of Us, On the Run from the American Dream, Psychopoetica, Retort Magazine, Samsdot Publishing, Shantytown Anomaly, Sidereality, Staplegun Press, Star*Line, Yellow Bat Review

Lazy Fascist Press
830 SW 18th Avenue
Portland, OR 97205

ISBN: 1-936383-16-0

THE FLAPPY PARTS

ONCE UPON A TIME

There was a man in my town
who danced
on rainbows,
bathed
in sunshine,
and sang to
bunnies in the park.

Authorities in charge
had to fuck him up

hardcore.

A LONG TIME AGO

we flying reptilian things warmed our hides
on sun-baked rocks before taking
to the sky in numbers.

primal stuff (later packaged as spam)
spewed from fissures in the earth
below.

we landed;
a voice from the sky said "eat."

we did and thus became
Man.

A LITTLE KNOWN FACT

Clouds were invented in 1894
by a man named Paul Weintraub.

Looking up at the sky one morning,
he felt something had to be put there
to break the monotony.

While the first clouds were little more
than crude tufts of cotton,
technology advanced with time,

bringing us the clouds
we know today.

MOTEL HELL

I am not, nor have I ever been, a rich man.

When traveling, I check in at only the seediest motels.

The last one I patronized was a plain, box-like structure advertised by a dead neon sign. It had iron bars on the windows. It was landscaped with long-dead shrubs. The guy at the counter wore a wife-beater, picked his nose and smelled of sardines.

The room he gave me was tiny, walls and floor covered with so much semen I didn't need a florescent light to see it—years and years worth of man-seed, piled on so thick I thought fossils might be buried between layers.

Perhaps a tag team of semen throwers had shared this room on multiple occasions. If so, I was staying at a place where famous men slept.

The possibility failed to excite. I fell onto the bed and into the disemboweled hooker on the comforter. Looked like she'd been rotting for weeks, but that neither surprised nor distressed me.

I don't expect quality housekeeping, wherever it is I may roam.

THIS JUST IN . . .

Today's polls indicate the nation at large
has gone completely and utterly insane.
When asked for their favorite president
9 out of 10 Americans chose "walrus."
The rest chose "pickled meats."

Cities now brim with madness.
Human heads roll laughing in gutters
as circus midgets emerge from graves
and karma wheels spin madly
across streets.

Better board your doors;
take immediate shelter;
stockpile enough food
and water to last
several weeks

because the weatherman and I
are stopping by for tea,
nude backgammon,
and chainsaw canasta
after the commercial man speaks.

WELCOME MAT

A school chum
called me yesterday
from out of the blue.

He said he wanted to
stop by, chat,
and catch up
on old times.

I responded by
drawing a skull
with testicles
hanging
from eye sockets,
which I then taped
to the front door.

Really don't want
to be reminded
of those times,
thank you very much.

LOVE COMES HARD

when your soulmate wants you to help
her pick out a new handbag
from the mall while you're busy
tripping on acid and experiencing
cosmic consciousness in the middle
of the dining room floor.

The tin foil wrapped around your head
to keep out government mind-beams
and harmful carcinogenic rays
doesn't help much, either.

**LICK THIS PAGE
FOR A HALLUCINOGENIC EFFECT**

CIGARETTE USE IS OFF-LIMITS FROM THIS POINT ON

or else my head will explode
in a stunning shower of debris
and the 87 different life forms
presently residing in my body
will disenfranchise themselves
from the shell that was once
my corporeal self and report back
to shady government agents
who have all the proper
documentation.

THE PERFECT LEADER

would be the robo-corpse of
*INSERT YOUR FAVORITE DEAD PRESIDENT
HERE*,
leading the country with
a constrictor's embrace
and a hyena's smile.

I can see him now
—speaking from a giant,
disembodied
horse head in the sky*

*(The object
his worshipers will
someday call
The Meat-Temple).

He ain't gonna be no guy
pushing sixty
so there'll be
no more masturbation
to Cold War fantasies.

(People will like that.)

He's young and
vibrant and ageless
so he's ready to
push for any change.

(People will like that, too.)

He knows
—as you don't
but someday will
—that the first nuclear winter
will see to it that all promises
are erased

as promised

on time

AN EVEN BETTER LEADER

would be a sentient black cube
forever spinning on a desk.
Never partial,
never judgmental,
it would just mete out retribution
whenever it saw fit.

YALTA (You'd think they might lay off a bit)

but shrapnel blew through flesh
the very moment
Stalin sipped his tea
and FDR removed a
cheese cracker
from the butler's plate.

FDR should have
plunged a knife in Stalin's
heart as Winston delivered
the chokehold from behind

(How loudly the National
Anthem would play!)

but he continued to chat and
pose for the seedy paparazzi
—all smiles for the public eye.

IF A GOVERNING BODY DROPPED A LARGE-SCALE THERMONUCLEAR DEVICE AND THEN HIGH-TAILED IT TO THE CELLAR WHERE THE CONCRETE IS A MILE THICK

they would
still address themselves
as Senator Roger and
Senator Tom

A DICTATOR REDECORATES

The executioner needs room
to dump bodies into zinc-lined coffins resting below.

Remember that when you install
the tabletop guillotines.

Oh yes... The Judas Chair...
How could I forget?

Could you place that below the overhead mirror?

THE MODERN DEBTOR'S PRISON

Since we are no longer allowed
to throw you in cuffs
and leg-chains
we'll endeavor to annoy you
into a very public insanity.

Please excuse us
—we have a courtesy call to make.

GO FIGURE

I went to the
job interview
still drunk
with a condom
clinging
to my nether-part.

I got there
on time
only because
I ran a few
red lights
and ignored
school crossings.

But I guess
I managed
to conceal
all that stuff

because
the-powers-that-be
handed me
the position
of Health and Safety Director
just two days later.

TIPS AND TRICKS ON DRIVING
– Excerpted From the Manuscripts of Chivega Tringpu (1230 - 1334)

* Insert not the key into the ignition. It goes against the Tao of the Road, and will cause the Fires of Tripanu to awaken in your car (e.g. it will explode).

* The steering wheel mocks the Watercourse Way. Use it not.

* Burn your maps; ask not for directions! The Tao of the Road will never misdirect you.

* The rigid and the inflexible obey traffic laws. Let your car flow, stream-like, through busy urban streets. Let it smash blissfully through the windows of Asian liquor stores.

* Beware, oh noble one! The drivers across from you are cannibalistic herukas that drink from skullcaps filled with blood!

* Finally, see to it that your tags aren't expired and that you carry your license and registration with you at all points along the space-time continuum.

LUNCH HOUR

The guy manning the deep fryer
at the burger joint
doesn't look too happy.

Perhaps I'm wrong
but it appears as though
he's sprinkling something
in the oil.

I think I'll wait and observe
the other patrons before
eating my food.

RUSH HOUR

There's a victim, and I'm going, and they're going and
everyone's going—teeth gnashing, balls banging,
temples throbbing. We lick our collective teeth and
shiver at the frisson of soon-to-be-bloodied enamel.

The victim tries his best to scream. It sounds
like a bubble arising from a filthy bog. He doesn't
have time to scream again. We're on top of him,
ripping away tendons, tearing away limbs. Our hands
claw through the mess we've made, and some of us
choke on it as we scarf the shit down.
But this shit is good shit; this shit is fine shit,
so we savor it while we can.

Work starts in an hour.

MULTIPLE MORNINGS

Morning One

My bowels feel heavy. I need to defecate.

The bathroom is a sty. I have no idea why there's so much shit smeared on the wall, ceiling, floor, even caked in the bathtub. Is this mine?

No matter. I take my seat and concentrate on empting my bowels.

Nothing exits.

INDIFFERENCE

Walt and Mary got hitched
forty-seven years prior
to their shared death in a car cash
just outside Nashville on I-40.

(Back then
the sex had at least been good.)

They didn't love each other,
but they didn't hate each other, either.

They merely tolerated each other's presence
until they were laid out together,
side by side in matching coffins.

GHOSTS

live
in forgotten
rooms

sound like
whispers
on a subway

VORTEX

I feel the black hole in me
growing wider.

Just yesterday I walked outside
and saw a flower growing by the porch.
I haven't seen flowers in ages;
perhaps I've never seen them at all.

I bent down to smell it.

Before I could smell anything,
the head of the flower
disappeared into my chest.

MOVE ON, NOTHING TO SEE HERE

WHEN I DREAM OF MINE ENEMIES

I do not ram a sawed-off
shotgun into their temples
or get creative with a saw
or any other type of
electrical device.

I don't kill them.

I don't even hurt them.

It's far better to put underwear
on their heads and throw them
out on the basketball court
in the middle of the game

and watch
as all the cheerleaders laugh
and laugh
and laugh.

PROTECTIVE COATING
with Pugnacious Jones

there's a protective coating over my nose and mouth.
it prevents the black oil from penetrating my defenses
and can also be used as a form of birth control
more reliable than the sponge
and oh my where'd i put my gun.
get it.
get that gun.
load it.
cock it.
fire it at will.
he's not a bad guy,
but deserves to die anyway.
thank you very much.
<crunch> <crunch> <irregular heartbeat> <fading>

THE COMMERCIALIZATION OF MR. DE LEON'S FOUNTAIN

Slip into
the fountain
one and all.
Let the years
fall away,
watch them peel
like old flesh.
Close your eyes;
remember the
halcyon days
of youth.
(Fields of poppies,
your first kiss.)
Defy the clock.
Give Father Time
a handshake
(or a stern slap
on the wrist).
Do this;
do more,
all for a mere
twenty dollar donation.
What a meager sum:
a dead president
exchanged
for ten minutes
of eternity.
Leave happy,
but don't forget
to come back.

We'll toss away the
lock for you
—and Sunday's are
always half-off.

IN A FACTORY TOWN

the scent
of sulfur,
acetone
and
garbage bins
will always
remind you
of tricycles,
june bugs
and
cicadas

SUMMER WIND

I leave the house
and the breeze assaults me,
leaving welts on my back
and bacteria on my crotch.

Sexually transmitted diseases
have gone airborne.

MULTIPLE MORNINGS
Morning Two

Something's stabbing my eyes. Didn't realize night ever happened, and I don't remember going to sleep. I try to stand, but cannot. It's as though whatever I'm lying on (linoleum; I'm on the kitchen floor) has bonded with my skin.

I take a seat in the closest chair and watch the blank TV. Seems like the least taxing thing to do, apart from maybe curling up in a fetal ball for a few days. I try to choose that option—just as an intellectual curiosity—but my body won't contort. It's too much hassle, so I sit on the chair and look at the floor, then the walls, then the ceiling.

ON A TYPICAL DAY

Comets
streak across
soup bowls.

Star clusters
congeal within
record grooves.

Wormholes
open inside
dresser drawers.

Nebulas
sprout between
theater aisles.

People
focus on
scuffed shoes.

WORST CASE SCENARIO

Benjamin Lybeck, age 54,
reclined in his living room
following a day spent
listening to employees
bitch about being too hot.

(His workers made air-conditioners—
the irony was not at all lost
—but they would trip over cords
and demand workman's comp
so fuck 'em.)

Just as he reached for a smoke
legions of the undead
broke through the door
and plowed headfirst
into the bay window.

(It seems Benjamin should
have been watching the news,
but the TV was flashing
video taped porn
at the worst possible time.)

In the end,
they ate his flesh with wild abandon
but saved his brain for a former employee
who later partook of it
with relish.

IN THE PEOPLE MUSEUM
Exhibit #4

The corporate types hang by their neckties
behind plexi-glass.

Did you know they think they're out to lunch
—much like the lion who believes his kingdom
is a twenty by twenty plot at the Zoo?

Watch them hop and bop.
How amusing!

They're convinced the cage is a brownstone near Wall Street
and that their secretary has nice breasts.

However...

We know they're really controlled
by the evil Puppet-Master ZILCORE.
It's only strings attached to cell-phones
that make plastic limbs move
and cellophane lips slap.

Read the note below the exhibit:

PLEASE DO NOT TELL THESE PEOPLE
WHAT LIES BEYOND THEIR CAGE.

I hear it's safer that way.

DEATH-IN-LIFE LOVE SONG

he raises silver
to plow red furrows
through warm peach
resistance

(force + pressure
= oblivion
colored rivers
flow over
safety glass smile)

pulsing rhythm
sings red tides
under hand

(painted lips
sown between
velvety walls
grin without source
only darkness lies
in empty cavities)

death-in-life love song
resonates through
organic strings

(grave dirt
pistons valves
the seat of love
cradled in new
cathedral
he bows

unworthy supplicant)

play these notes
filtered through
foreign blood
—medicinal miracle
pulsing warm reminders
in his hand

HOLIDAY

Something stares at me from behind a red-framed window set in nothing—ZANTA KLAWX. Yes, that's its name, a god-like moniker that would call down the heavens if spoken aloud.

But no, it's not ZANTA KLAWX himself. It's a life-size plastic model, lit with an interior bulb. The warm glow softens plastic features. I lose myself in them, dreaming of wrapping paper and winter nights at home.

I pull back when I sense something wrong within the model, something the 60-watt bulb inside can't illuminate, something that has no relation to gentle memories and stinks of death.

The window opens. ZANTA's mouth widens and, with great suction, pulls me into the belly of what must be a huge compacting machine.

Walls of regret close in on me, tighter and tighter.

PARANOIA POEMS

I. Eureka!

I can finally prove
the neighbor's apartment
is filled with
whirling recording devices
and bleeping gizmos
of every make and model.

II. One Day

I got really drunk
and threw up in a corner.
Looking down at my vomit,
I watched alien life forms writhe
in a sea of gastric acid
and partially digested toast.

TWO BUS POEMS

I. On the Greyhound

you get to meet dozens of people
you'll never want to see again
—but they tend to be forgotten easily enough
once they reach wherever it is they're going.

Come to think of it,
riding this wave
is a lot like
traveling Greyhound.

There's no seatbelt
and people lean their heads
against windows
watching scenery pass by.

II. Greyhell

Some part of me
loves the crazy man
next to me, loves
the irate bus driver,
and loves every
monotonous inch
of the road.

It loves them
even as the seat
seeps disease
like an Indian blanket

and old men breathe
respiratory sickness
into the air.

CATHODE RAY WATCHER

The TV pumps astral-images into my mind
that I decode and recode.
It transmits, accepts and rejects.
Older models just transmit.

I have a top-of-the-line model.

My brain has a user interface
that's interfaced
each time I sit in front of the screen.
It doesn't matter if the TV's off.

My brain is a top-of-the-line model, too.

SCENE FROM THE LATE-LATE SHOW

>beginning of scene<

An elderly farmer is giving mouth-to-mouth
resuscitation to a pig when his wife comes out and
bangs him to death with a hammer because she thinks
he's having carnal relations when, in fact, he is
saving the pig's life.

Both the elderly farmer and the pig die. The wife,
after having disposed of the bodies in a wood
shredder, shoots herself to death in the kitchen. The
camera lingers long and heavy over red walls and brain
matter.

>end of scene<

WHEN YOU RUN YOUR FINGERS ACROSS A CREMATORIUM WALL

you leave a thumbprint
in the residue
of organic waste,
in the memories
of flesh (passion)
of bone (structure)
and sinew (acts)
so easily rubbed off.

OTHERS

There are those
who wish others ill.

There are those
who love plants
like people.

There are those
who wear their
pants inside out
and their tongues
against their shoes.

There are those
to whom
matter
is but a dream,

and destruction
is creation
in reverse.

TABLEAU FOR THE 25th

Nothing adhered to anything.

Everything shot out in spirals from the floor,
entering the ceiling at an obtuse angle.

Radiant specters danced from the ceiling
and made love to my TV-watching corpse.

My corpse writhed and buckled on the couch,
but that was due to the maggots inside

roosting like chickens.

BUG

He watches the bug

tiny
exoskeleton
encased
vessel
of
oblivion

scurry into its hole of

safe
dark
quiet
nothingness.

Man arises

jealous
needing
probing.

Only his finger fits.

MULTIPLE MORNINGS
Morning Three

In lieu of anything better, I stand in the center of the living room. I could spin left. I could spin right. I could take a step forward or a step back. Or I could do none of these things, which, for the moment, seems like the one true option. Everything's nice and calm when I remain motionless. Nothing confusing happens. Thoughts don't spin.

Time just passes me by.

TWO PERSPECTIVES

(Inside the Tunnel):

Whistles mean nothing to a man
who is tired and needs rest.

(Outside the Tunnel):

Sunlight reflects off
a flesh-filled grille.

THE EMPTY MAUSOLEUM

There was once a rich man
who bought a small
South Pacific island
so he alone
might reside in all the splendor
money could afford.

He built a grand house,
erected towering statuary,
and ordered skilled laborers
to design a marble mausoleum
where his remains
might later be stored.

When he died, however,
he died alone,
and the caviar in the cooler spoiled
and soon turned green.

Years later,
wrapped in silken bed-sheets,
his flesh fell away as the
plaster cracked

in his home by the sea.

15%

Brains sizzle
sausage-like
on the grill.

This restaurant.
will eat you.

It will suck
your blood.

Leave a tip;
walk away.

The door
smacks you
as you leave.

AT THE TECHNOLOGY STORE

I didn't realize the computer
was a Fellation-XSL model
until I sat down to use it.

The hard drive
was really hard that day.

My, oh my.

It took me to the stars
and the bars
and back again,

twice.

It sucked away pieces of my soul
and did not return them.

Other customers had used it,
and I wondered if their soul-pieces
churned with mine
—turning on and off like photons
inside that sweet processor of sin.

I HAVE FREE WILL, DAMN YOU!

I'm afraid
that's not what
our thermal pod sensors
indicate.

They know more than you
concerning such matters.

Don't worry;
take a deep breath.

Let the mainframe take over.

COMPUTERSTADT

I like this
bio-molecular headgear
—it suits me well.

I also like the feel
of the dual-sensors
lodged in the sockets
where my eyes used to rest.

(Each bleeping gizmo
is like a piece of my own body
—so supple, so right.)

I enjoy being wired to the mainframe.

It's pleasurable to exist in stasis.

No one bothers me and I can be happy

—just as long as the scientists
program positive memories into my chip
and don't drink too much
the night before.

LoSt in ThE PATTeRNS

Now:

ball bustin' girlies
plentiful beefcakes throbbin'
ass slappin'/playin'
feelin' dancin'
yessss!

Later:

friggin' grando doobie spliff
ummmmmmmm...
rollin' pukin' talkin' askin'
oooooooooh...
beautific fucks/meditational farts
hell yeah!

Ultimately:

(death)

BROUGHT TO YOU BY

I woke up today only to find
my organic operating system
had been sponsored by
Omni-Corp.

I tried—and tried valiantly
—but couldn't think of anything
without first seeing logos
flash before my eyes.

I thought I was alone in this misery
until I made a few phone calls
and realized my friends and neighbors
had experienced the same phenomena.

But they didn't seem to mind,
and that only complicated the problem.

THE CHATTERING THINGS

The things in my head
are plotting their escape.
They intend to take three-quarters
of my brain on the way out,
leaving me with just enough gray matter
to breathe and, when necessary, wet myself.
They will slide out of my life
on slick and diaphanous pseudopods,
enter the brains of those who claim to know me,
and share with them all my mundane secrets.
Ultimately, they will impart info
to men in crisp suits and dark glasses
who will twist and turn my thoughts
until harmless fantasies are rendered
unstable, seditious and unpatriotic.
The phone will ring off the hook—
friends, relatives, spooks
—but I'll be in no condition to answer.
I'll just remain on the floor,
gurgling and wetting myself
until whatever happens
happens.

UNCERTAINTY

I stand outside on the corner
doing seriously drug-related things.

Every eye is turned in my direction.

Twitch, twitch, twitch.

I know I'm making too much noise;
the neighbors are surely awake.

Doors slam.

Did I just slam those doors?

Not sure.

THE FLAPPY PARTS

I need a Big Mac,
a filet of fish,
tobacco
and a Fire-Pleasure Meal—

a mouth
big enough
to fit all this

—spare ribs,
murder and
rape-sandwiches,
mirrors
and big
red bongs.

Gimme
Gimme
Gimme
or I'll become
a flapping
skeleton.

I'm already
losing control
over my
joints.

MULTIPLE MORNINGS
Morning Four

Perhaps I should eat something. Can't say I'm hungry, but I don't remember the last time I ate.

I open the freezer door. Inside: a bunch of denuded skulls in baggies. A few still have flesh remaining. They must be ... leftovers.

Maybe it's best to just think about eating.

I think very hard, and recall a dense, hard-to-swallow cereal foisted upon me in my youth. I imagine I'm eating that. It fails to satisfy. Dinner, I'm sure, will be just as dire. The mind-steak, overcooked, the dream-potatoes, lumpy.

ALL'S FAIR IN LOVE AND WAR

We weren't in it
for the sex.
Ours was a true love,
but that didn't end
the war
or raise
battle-scarred dead
or give names
to millions buried
in mass graves
or left to rot
in the sun.

Babies still
decomposed
in the arms
of their mothers
and left organic
Rorschach patterns
to stain the ground
with the broth
of their
decay.

(Wait...

Caroline
—I think her name was
Caroline.)

PERRY MASON, WHERE ARE YOU?

Come on, Perry—we need you.

I know you're dead, but you must have
supernatural powers from beyond the grave.

God'll let you come back, and when you do
you'll be better than ever.

Just ask Him. He can't say no.

Melt those whores with your X-Ray eyes.
Punish 'em all—fuck 'em to hell and back.

The world needs you, Perry. We're all going to die.

But you do nothing;
you're just paper and celluloid and
a collection of childhood dreams.

ON MY BIRTHDAY

She brings me breakfast in bed
and a newspaper,
little things designed
to help me forget,
but I still remember
the red in her smile
and the safety glass in her hair.

I say nothing;
I don't move until she leaves.

I eat the food,
and it has no flavor.
I pick up the newspaper,
and it slides through my hands.

LOW MAINTENANCE

I need the perfect wife
—a woman who knows
I love her even if
I don't say it every year.

She must realize
that less is more
and love isn't found
in sugar-words
or dime-a-dozen gifts
stored in warehouses
near Sheboygan.

In the morning, I'll
pass by the kitchen and wave.

She'll think: "I know he loves
me because he waved at me
today."

I'll think: "I know she loves
me because she returned
my wave."

And then I'll fly out the door.

IN A BETTER WORLD

Mary Poppins will take us to her fairy tale hideaway
where we will dance with succulent fawns
who speak some Finnish dialect.

GETTING BACK

I rammed the needle
into the bug's head
and savored the pop
as its protective bubble
burst.

(A little bored now.)

I inserted the firecracker
between the frog's legs
and shielded my eyes
from the debris.
(red and yellow
—colors are richest
when they're
organic.)

(Time for ritual.)

I burned the beehive and
inhaled the smoke/inhaled the bees
and lifted my arms to the
gods I had lost.
(arms become roadmaps
of insect suicide
—pain beats the drum
of all homecomings.)

(Payoff)

And they smiled down
so that I might recall
those jocund days.

ONLY COLDER

for El Greco

I stand

beside images
of sanctified dust
and stare into the faces
of icons, saints
and holy-men

(eyes can't connect
when the source of
all knowledge is
stone)

I trace

my finger through
the dust
to unleash a storm
of gray swirls

(watch them twist on stoic faces)

I marvel

their bodies are
no different
than my own

AN EXPERIENCE BEYOND WORDS

I gave names to universes
as eternity danced
the light fanspastic
on the edge of a thumbnail.

My body bubbled like magma
and flowed like water.

I became star-stuff.

Black holes spilled
from my vagina
in bountiful profusion

(and I'm not even a girly.)

TRANSMISSION #4

So much blood on the streets;
crazy slimy things darting
into bus stations and alleyways.

They're trying to kill us.
Always trying to kill us.

They're aware of the transmitters
in our heads. The ones that call out
to parts unknown.

Parts unknown haven't answered yet,
but I'm confident they will soon.

'Give it time,' Dr. Rasmussen told me.
I'm not even sure who Dr. Rasmussen is.
He just floats around in a red mist,
has a mouth of a thousand stars,

and that's all I know.

GRANNY BE MINE

Granny loves me; I love her.
She connects me to my past
and makes me forget I was ever insane.

I hold her and love her.

I take her into my arms
and slide her down my throat.
I feel her squirming down in my belly,
but she doesn't want out.

She likes it there;
it makes her feel like an infant again.

Earlier, she told me
she wanted me to cook and
eat her after she dies.
She saw something about
African tribes doing that
on the Discovery Channel
and found it really touching.

(Wait...
Granny never said anything like that.)

STANDARDIZED GOVT. SAFETY FILM
(#1343)

START: (... in the center,
screaming.)

Just found something...
AWWWHHHH SHIT!!!!
(That was something I didn't want to find!)

Done some bad things... Where am I?

(The nurse said something about
Room 17.)

I was told I'd fit in here
'cause I never keep it practical.

(Weird stuff has a way of slipping in
like an outside tongue filling a mouth.)

Wait...
The wall is making noises again
—bad omens for a tin-penny.

(But worse stuff happens during shake-moments.
—Hey, I think this is a shake-moment!)

BEGIN SHAKE MOMENT:
I'm finally convinced that (to take a) life is bad.

(This is basic level functioning.)

Touching leads to sin. Sin is tactile. I'm tactile, too.

(Just bits STREAMMMMMMMING together.)

Balance

=== the secret of...

Balance

=== the answer why...

(It all comes straight from the
fundamental processing unit
of the brain.)

Now,
I
understand.

(This is TRUE and this is FALSE.
Here are your TRUE and FALSE hats...)

But is knowledge sinful?
And how about (information withheld)?
Or (information withheld)?

(Perhaps I'm speaking-in-tongues.
Have I been screaming for an hour now?)

Nope. It's all just mental attack.

(This was never part of the agreement.)

To hell with it! All I know is this:

THAT THING
COULDN'T HAVE COME
FROM THIS UNIVERSE!

(Do most people see this?
Gag... so much decaying flesh!)

END: (*NOTE TO TRANSLATOR: Find out what this all
means.*)

MULTIPLE MORNINGS
Morning Five

I stand in front of the mirror, naked, and can't stop staring at my body, so scrawny and disgusting, like something that might blow away with the wind or come up from the earth. And my eyes, like dim lights submerged in dirt. I look like I should be in pain, or at least in a state of profound malaise. But I'm numb. I touch my fingers together. There is no sensation.

I look past myself, at the room reflected behind me: The window. I could dive out of it for a quick yet rewarding descent. The closet. I could hang myself with a belt.

I leave the bedroom, en route to the kitchen. The stove. After putting my head in, I could luxuriate for as long as it takes. The freezer. It would take longer, but would give me time to crystallize my thoughts.

TELEVISED CONFUSION

The Discovery Channel is airing
a special about survival soon.

It deals with how one might make
it (partially unscathed) if the world
were to flip its proverbial shit
and go to hell in an equally
proverbial handbasket.

It all makes me wonder what
the illuminati has under its sleeve.

I would watch the damn thing, but I fear
THEY would spread disinformation
through the airwaves. For example:
"In the wake of a biochemical
attack, please breath heavily."

The TV is a multi-eyed devouring beast,
you know.

KEEPSAKE

The thing lies in a heap, like a bag filled with jelly. It gurgles and bubbles just inside the door where people see it slouching. It's been there for years, I'm not sure from whence it came. Could be that I found it in a box underground, or at my grandfather's funeral when I was ten.

On Wednesday it started to rustle, to click and pop and squeal. I pretend it's the TV, but sleep never comes. My skin sags, my breath reeks, and my skull gleams beneath the skin. Perhaps I should get rid of it—scoop the thing up, dump it in a hole, open windows now stuck to the sill.

But there's a certain attachment to the things of the past. I can't throw it away. If I do, I'll forget who I am.

DOWN WHERE IT'S DARK

I have
no idea
who I am
or who I
used to be
or why
I've spent
so long
between
these walls
maybe
I was waiting
for something
maybe
I forgot

DENIAL

"Can't you see she still loves me!"
screamed the man.
Sheathed in white,
his new jacket wrapped around
and buckled in the back
securely.
Hollow-eyed,
leather brown,
his lover smiled back
a toothy, gaping rictus.

A WARNING

don't trust the person
bearing gifts

      for he may be
      bad (white/black/yellow/orange/purple) man

waiting in bushes,
laughing forever.

SUNDAY PARANOIA

Preacher Mike was
so friendly
I thought he might be planning
my death.

He asked for my e-mail address
after the service ended

and I knew the gig was up.

I THOUGHT U WAS A HOLY ONE
with Shaina K. Donihe (age 11)

God loves the children of the world.
Red
yellow
black
and blue
...He loves them all.

I am a blessed pig.

The Bible tells me
I am weak but He is strong
and that Jesus loves me.
Hallelujah.
Amen.
Praise God.

I am a holy and blessed pig.

PAUPA, NEW GUINEA

Puppet shows
make the natives
smile
—but they're unaware
of the plot

devised in secret

thousands of miles
away.

FUGUE POEMS

I. Nonsense and Re-sense

Liquid crystal crap on the magnet southwise turned below the
equinox belt
Timid squirrel-mouse shimmering in the
noonday sun
Lonely mother attic blues
Green facepaint streaked holiday
glistening for no one
but itself.

II. Four Things I Love

89 cent cookies
homeless men
mad cow disease
food grade clones

IS IT REALLY THIS BAD?

The billboards turn my brain
into candy
and I am held
in their erotic sway.

Sometimes I forget about driving.

I've only killed three pedestrians
in seventeen years on the road.

Hell, they should have been
driving a car
in the first place.

A REALLY WEIRD SHOW

I saw this sitcom
where the mother
returned home
to tend to her
precocious children
after a day
spent working
for the man
at the pizza parlor.

The only difference
was that she
now had a huge
gunshot wound
to the chest.

(A victim of armed robbery,
I guess.)

The children snickered
and then cracked up
as the mother scowled
disapprovingly and the
laugh track roared.

I think it only lasted one season.

YEARS FROM NOW

We do things
as you do things
—our separate lives
are quite compatible
if you dig
beneath the surface.

Our cars may fly
but they still break down
and people continue
to kick them
while faces grow bright
as flames from jetpacks.

Our buildings may float
on antimatter seas,
but that doesn't mean
paint never cracks
or that ceilings
never leak.

We may communicate
with telepathy
and send e-mail
via mind beam
but wires continue to cross
and faces still flush red.

Nothing has really changed—
the world still revolves and spins
—though we no longer
breathe air

and bathrooms exist only
in the past.

IT WAS A NORMAL, OZONE-FILLED DAY IN EARLY JULY

My next-door neighbors were having a loud conversation
about nothing in particular and smoking cigars I smelled
from ten yards away.

The stupid teenager across the street was mowing
the grass with his shirt off, drinking beer
and listening to a walkman,

and I was standing on my porch wishing the neighborhood
would just blow away when the thing fell from the sky
and covered the road with mush.

It looked like a huge praying mantis—ten feet long and
glistening black.
Segmented legs kicked at the air and its carapace gleamed:
a dark diamond in the sun.

The neighbors gathered around as it shook and quivered.
I too moved in for a closer look, interacting with these people
for the first time in ages.

I grimaced at the smell of cooking meat and melting plastic.
It took all my will to refrain from vomiting half-digested
lunch atop the terrible, twitching thing.

A label was affixed to the side of its head:
GOVERNMENT PROPERTY
it said, followed by a string of alien characters below a mouth
that looked suspiciously like an organic recording device.

A lot of pictures were taken, but they were confiscated by
men in dark suits and darker glasses who arrived
in black helicopters to clean up the mess.

A day later, my next-door neighbors were having the same
loud conversation
about nothing in particular and smoking cigars I smelled
from ten yards away.

The stupid teenager across the street was mowing
the grass, still shirtless, still drinking beer,
still listening to music.

Yet I remained inside—downstairs windows secured,
chest of drawers in front of the door—as I awaited
the bullet earned for knowing just a little too much.

ON THE LAST DAY

I WORE:

(inside): A white sleeveless undershirt
Striped boxers w/ logo-imprinted waistband
White socks

(outside): Checkered button-up shirt
Blue, pleated trousers
Sensible shoes

I ATE:

An egg-salad sandwich—butter on the side
A bowl of cold cereal

I LATER DRANK:

Coffee—extra strong

I THOUGHT:

Everything was OK

I WENT:

To work and made a lot of money

I FUCKED:

My secretary

AFTER WORK:

I was consumed in a holocaust of pure fire

AND THEN:

Nothing

MULTIPLE MORNINGS
Final Morning

Today, I'm going to eat something real. Scrambled eggs. Can't remember the last time I ate them, or even if I had the same name and face then.

Maybe this'll be the start of a grand new day.

When I crack the shells, whites are cloudy and the yolks are almost green. I put them on the stove and shake the skillet for hours. Half the eggs are burnt to a crisp, the other half, barely cooked.

There's no use eating. There's no real food. Closing my eyes, I imagine myself entombed in a sepulcher. People stare down at me. The lid closes. Darkness. I can't see the outside of the sarcophagus, but know it's covered head-to-toe with bats.

THE SECRET

The only way to
avoid the madness
—the leeching,
ever-encroaching
madness—
is to be a madman
yourself.

Therein lies the balance.
You can't even hope
to travel the road
any other way

and we're going to
drive until this
road ends

somewhere in Paducah.

TRANSFIGURATION

My machine
is powered up
and ready to go.
Feel it rumble
between my legs;
feel it gyrate
in that place
known only
by the gods.
This is
the seat of truth;
this is where
divinity lies.
Turn me on
via remote control,
open me up
from within.
Step up to me,
take the baggage
from my eyes,

carry me home.

ONE FINE DAY

we forgot our jobs
and our place
in the corporate hierarchy
and, upon finishing dinner,
ran outside to find the ghosts
we knew were hiding
in Granny's barn.

ACTUAL RE-CODING CONVERSATION
Colorado Springs, CO – 06/07/04

>Phone rings>
>Line opens>

VOICE #1: To whom am I speaking?

VOICE #2: I'm being bang-raped at the corner of Academy and Carefree . . .

VOICE #1: Excuse me?

VOICE #2: ...bang-raped by aggressively procrasturbating sesquipedalians.

VOICE #1: I don't know what you're talking about.

VOICE #2: Come get me, before it's too late.

VOICE #1: When will it be too late?

VOICE #2: Right now.

VOICE #1: Then I'll never make it in time.

VOICE #2: Not if you ignore physical laws and traffic lights.

VOICE #1: I don't even know you, sir.

VOICE #2: Yes, you do.

VOICE #1: No, I don't.

VOICE #2: Your voice sounds so familiar.

VOICE #1: Yours doesn't.

VOICE #2: Didn't we travel overseas together?

VOICE #1: No.

VOICE #2: Check out the same banned books from the library?

VOICE #1: Not to my knowledge.

VOICE #2: Didn't we once meet a man who called himself 'Chadwick Tate?'

VOICE #1: Drawing a blank, sorry.

VOICE #2: He had a deep red voice and copious facial scars. The nature of his implants set him apart from the crowd.

VOICE #1: Never laid eyes on him.

VOICE #2: But I know we've met before. Remember when Pablo gave me those folders, and then you had to—fuck! Another jet just flew by!

VOICE #1: Was it as black as the others?

VOICE #2: How did you know about the other jets?

VOICE #1: A little birdie told me.

VOICE #2: So, you do know what's going on!

VOICE #1: Perhaps.

VOICE #2: Can you tell me if Pablo's okay? I've been worried about him.

VOICE #1: No.

VOICE #2: That figures.

VOICE #1: But you can tell me how many jets you've seen today. Did their numbers increase?

VOICE #2: Why should I tell you?

VOICE #1: I need to update my records.

VOICE #2: I really can't say; there were too many of them to count.

VOICE #1: Did the sky look like it was filled with ants?

VOICE #2: Yes.

VOICE #1: That's all I need to know.

VOICE #2: Nothing else?

VOICE #1: Just make note of this conversation in your log, and then proceed according to plan.

VOICE #2: Yes, sir! Right away, sir!

VOICE #1: And don't fuck things up this time.

VOICE #2: Aye, aye, sir! Aye, aye, sir! Aye, aye, sir!

>VOICE #1 hangs up>

>VOICE #2 turns on, tunes in, and drops both in and out at the same time>

THE LAST DAY OF STASIS

I. Wake Up Call

Ah shit! Time to go to work! I loathe work. It blows the fetid corpses of disease-ravaged primates. I'd love to spend my entire day on the sofa as tantalizing machines create sex-love and fuck-kill dioramas in front of the curio cabinet.

But, alas, no machines for the wicked! Not today. Not ever. The dioramas are all in my head, but that's okay. Head-things are often pleasant and sometimes cool. I've been working on crystallizing a few them. It takes a lot of concentration, more than I have at the moment. So far I've only been able to project shadows of shadows that flicker and die.

II. Dissatisfaction

My job makes me want to kill myself, but I love it just the same. I love it for the security it brings me, and for the way it gets me in touch with the mechanical gears that run my life.

I want the machine to become a part of me. I want to feel its circuits pulse like a cock. I want it to ride me bareback, straight into the heart of the Arizona desert.

There, I will remember all the things I've forgotten.

III. Lunch Break

The refrigerator handle pulses lightly in my grip. I open it and withdraw a fleshy jug of milk. The jug scowls disapprovingly, but I drink from it anyway. I'm used to its antics.

110

I wipe my lips with my sleeve and taste old milk, dead milk, milk long forgotten, milk memorable only for its stench. The new milk goes down all harsh and chalky. I wonder what might be in it. Then I dismiss the question entirely. I've taken tons of filthy things into my body.

IV. A Religious Encounter

After work, Jesus and I drink coffee at the local Starbucks. It tastes like reheated tapwater, colored with brown food coloring, but I don't care. I'm talking with Jesus and that's all that matters.

He tells me not to fear, but that's easier said than done. Later, at my apartment, he makes me a buttercrest sandwich. I've never heard of a buttercrest sandwich, but I eat just the same. I figure if the messiah made it, it has to be good.

But he went a little heavy on the mayo.

V. Finally Alone

My balls are tender due to incessant whacking. I don't want to do it anymore. It feels like my soul is coming out of my penis, like the very essence of life is spilling out onto that old, old sock.

But I can't help myself; I'm a lifelong procrasturbator.

VI. End of the Day

I want to get high, but I'm all out of cough syrup. Dammit. I need that temporal displacement now more than ever. I need to close my eyes and watch the fractal geometry explode. I need to astral travel to the Everglades.

Death and fucking. Madness and cheese. There's nothing left for me here but magpie delight. I don't even know what magpie delight is. I'm guessing it's some kind of candy. Some kind of evil candy that sinks its claws into its victims' minds and removes their thoughts and fucks them when they're asleep and vulnerable.

VII. In Dreams

Monsters everywhere.

Doors closing when they shouldn't close. Heaviness in the air.

Monsters, monsters, monsters.

VIII. Clockwork Winding

I wake up to screams so high-pitched they sound electronic. A strange thing hangs from my mouth. It looks like a cable. A rather large one, strangely cock-like. I'm not sure where I picked it up, but it doesn't matter. I've woken up with stranger things connected to my body.

I grease up my crotch and armpits, slip into my clothes and put a freshening mint in my mouth. My breath feels alive and tingly but, really, there's nothing alive or tingly here. Then I head off to the car.

IX. Change of Pace

Gotta break this; gotta kill this. Can't take much more. Bills, bills, bills. Worry, worry, worry. The nagging friends and family. The taunts and the curses. Work, work, work. Where has the Zen gone, baby?

And so I jump into my car's (human?) hide-covered seats and insert glisteningly phallic keys into the vagina-slot. It accepts the offering with a quiver and makes groan-sex sounds. Then it's OFF! Oh my god yes, yes, yes! Flying down the roadway at a million miles a minute. Old greyhaired ladies look like streaky blobs in the nano-seconds before they pass beneath my wheels. Old men look like flapbutter pancakes spread from one side of the road to the other, stacked hundreds of layers high.

X. Closing Thoughts

It's all fun and games until people get hurt. I fucked around with fire-pleasure and got fire-pleasure, which turned to fire-fucking, which turned to fire-death, which turned to life-with-out-end.

And so here I am.

Going to slide into the womb now, slide free and clear into the zone before zones began. The Mother will welcome me into her soft and mushy arms. I will plant a kiss on her fetid green face as she makes the grave all snug and cozy for me. She will plant flowers by my head, and my decay will cause them to grow big and strong.

This is my last day of stasis.

ABOUT THE AUTHOR

Kevin Donihe, perhaps the world's oldest living wombat, resides in the hills of Tennessee. He is the Wonderland Award-winning author of House of Houses, Washer Mouth: The Man Who Was a Washing Machine, and several other books. His short fiction and poetry has appeared in The Mammoth Book of Legal Thrillers, ChiZine, The Cafe Irreal, Poe's Progeny, Bathtub Gin, Not One of Us, Dreams and Nightmares, Electric Velocipede, Bust Down the Door and Eat All the Chickens, The Magazine of Bizarro Fiction, and many other venues.

Bizarro books

CATALOG   SPRING 2010

Bizarro Books publishes under the following imprints:

RAW DOG SCREAMING PRESS

www.rawdogscreamingpress.com

www.eraserheadpress.com

www.afterbirthbooks.com

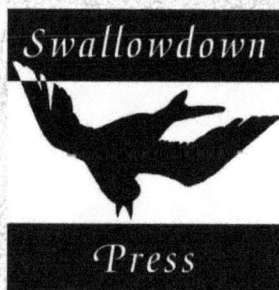

Swallowdown Press

www.swallowdownpress.com

For all your Bizarro needs visit:

WWW.BIZARROCENTRAL.COM

Introduce yourselves to the bizarro genre and all of its authors with the Bizarro Starter Kit series. Each volume features short novels and short stories by ten of the leading bizarro authors, designed to give you a perfect sampling of the genre for only $5 plus shipping.

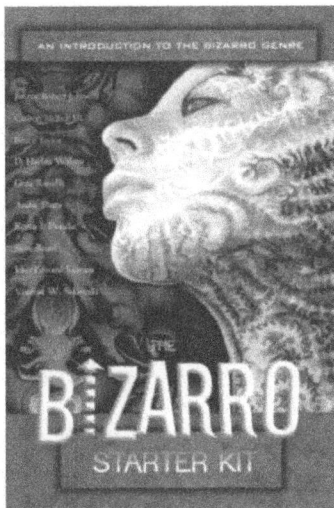

BB-0X1
"The Bizarro Starter Kit"
(Orange)

Featuring D. Harlan Wilson, Carlton Mellick III, Jeremy Robert Johnson, Kevin L Donihe, Gina Ranalli, Andre Duza, Vincent W. Sakowski, Steve Beard, John Edward Lawson, and Bruce Taylor.

236 pages $5

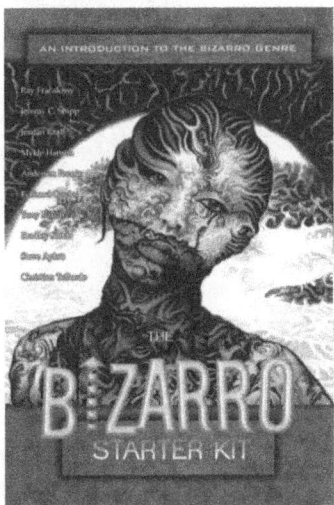

BB-0X2
"The Bizarro Starter Kit"
(Blue)

Featuring Ray Fracalossy, Jeremy C. Shipp, Jordan Krall, Mykle Hansen, Andersen Prunty, Eckhard Gerdes, Bradley Sands, Steve Aylett, Christian TeBordo, and Tony Rauch.

244 pages $5

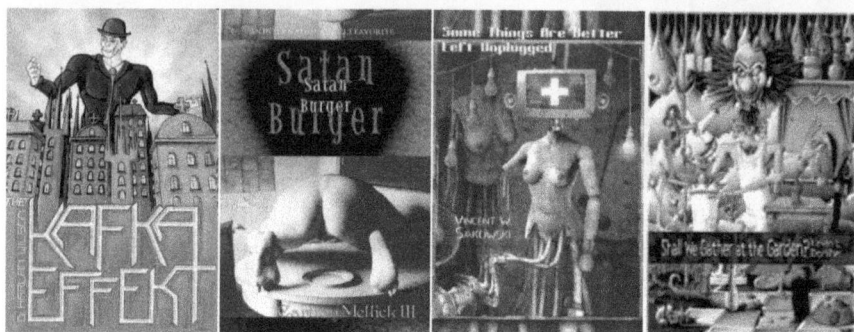

BB-001 "The Kafka Effekt" D. Harlan Wilson - A collection of forty-four irreal short stories loosely written in the vein of Franz Kafka, with more than a pinch of William S. Burroughs sprinkled on top. **211 pages $14**

BB-002 "Satan Burger" Carlton Mellick III - The cult novel that put Carlton Mellick III on the map ... Six punks get jobs at a fast food restaurant owned by the devil in a city violently overpopulated by surreal alien cultures. **236 pages $14**

BB-003 "Some Things Are Better Left Unplugged" Vincent Sakwoski - Join The Man and his Nemesis, the obese tabby, for a nightmare roller coaster ride into this postmodern fantasy. **152 pages $10**

BB-004 "Shall We Gather At the Garden?" Kevin L Donihe - Donihe's Debut novel. Midgets take over the world, The Church of Lionel Richie vs. The Church of the Byrds, plant porn and more! **244 pages $14**

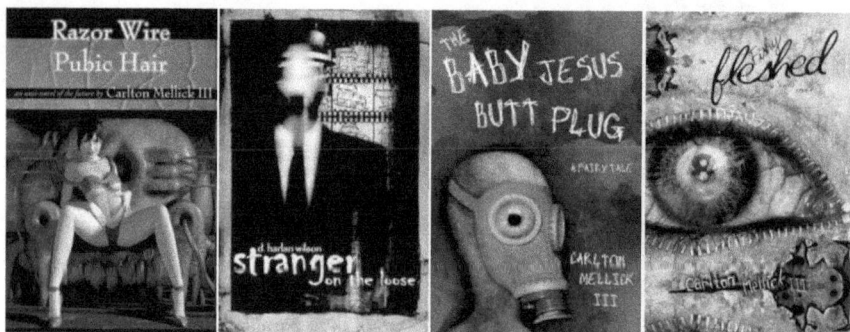

BB-005 "Razor Wire Pubic Hair" Carlton Mellick III - A genderless humandildo is purchased by a razor dominatrix and brought into her nightmarish world of bizarre sex and mutilation. **176 pages $11**

BB-006 "Stranger on the Loose" D. Harlan Wilson - The fiction of Wilson's 2nd collection is planted in the soil of normalcy, but what grows out of that soil is a dark, witty, otherworldly jungle... **228 pages $14**

BB-007 "The Baby Jesus Butt Plug" Carlton Mellick III - Using clones of the Baby Jesus for anal sex will be the hip sex fetish of the future. **92 pages $10**

BB-008 "Fishyfleshed" Carlton Mellick III - The world of the past is an illogical flatland lacking in dimension and color, a sick-scape of crispy squid people wandering the desert for no apparent reason. **260 pages $14**

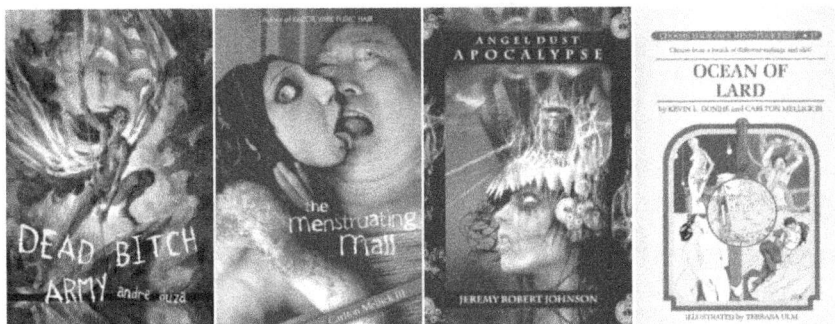

BB-009 "Dead Bitch Army" Andre Duza - Step into a world filled with racist teenagers, cannibals, 100 warped Uncle Sams, automobiles with razor-sharp teeth, living graffiti, and a pissed-off zombie bitch out for revenge. **344 pages $16**

BB-010 "The Menstruating Mall" Carlton Mellick III - "The Breakfast Club meets Chopping Mall as directed by David Lynch." - Brian Keene **212 pages $12**

BB-011 "Angel Dust Apocalypse" Jeremy Robert Johnson - Meth-heads, man-made monsters, and murderous Neo-Nazis. "Seriously amazing short stories..." - Chuck Palahniuk, author of Fight Club **184 pages $11**

BB-012 "Ocean of Lard" Kevin L Donihe / Carlton Mellick III - A parody of those old Choose Your Own Adventure kid's books about some very odd pirates sailing on a sea made of animal fat. **176 pages $12**

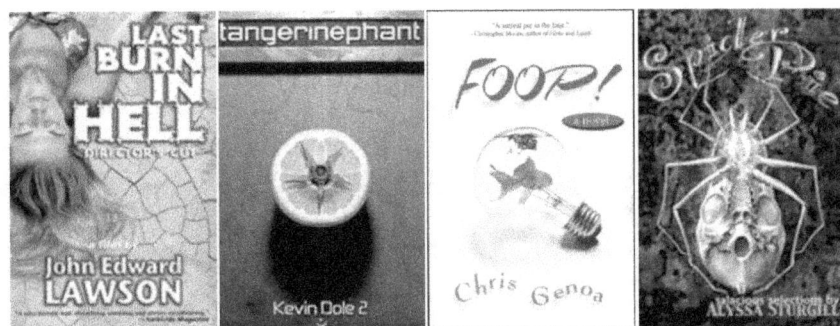

BB-013 "Last Burn in Hell" John Edward Lawson - From his lurid angst-affair with a lesbian music diva to his ascendance as unlikely pop icon the one constant for Kenrick Brimley, official state prison gigolo, is he's got no clue what he's doing. **172 pages $14**

BB-014 "Tangerinephant" Kevin Dole 2 - TV-obsessed aliens have abducted Michael Tangerinephant in this bizarro combination of science fiction, satire, and surrealism. **164 pages $11**

BB-015 "Foop!" Chris Genoa - Strange happenings are going on at Dactyl, Inc, the world's first and only time travel tourism company.

"A surreal pie in the face!" - Christopher Moore **300 pages $14**

BB-016 "Spider Pie" Alyssa Sturgill - A one-way trip down a rabbit hole inhabited by sexual deviants and friendly monsters, fairytale beginnings and hideous endings. **104 pages $11**

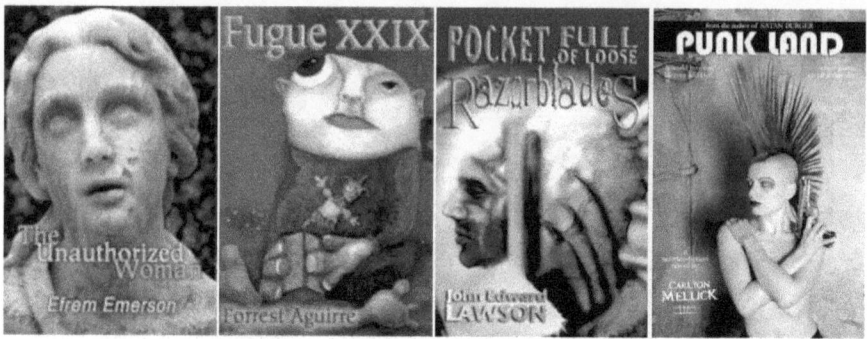

BB-017 "The Unauthorized Woman" Efrem Emerson - Enter the world of the inner freak, a landscape populated by the pre-dead and morticioners, by cockroaches and 300-lb robots. **104 pages $11**

BB-018 "Fugue XXIX" Forrest Aguirre - Tales from the fringe of speculative literary fiction where innovative minds dream up the future's uncharted territories while mining forgotten treasures of the past. **220 pages $16**

BB-019 "Pocket Full of Loose Razorblades" John Edward Lawson - A collection of dark bizarro stories. From a giant rectum to a foot-fungus factory to a girl with a biforked tongue. **190 pages $13**

BB-020 "Punk Land" Carlton Mellick III - In the punk version of Heaven, the anarchist utopia is threatened by corporate fascism and only Goblin, Mortician's sperm, and a blue-mohawked female assassin named Shark Girl can stop them. **284 pages $15**

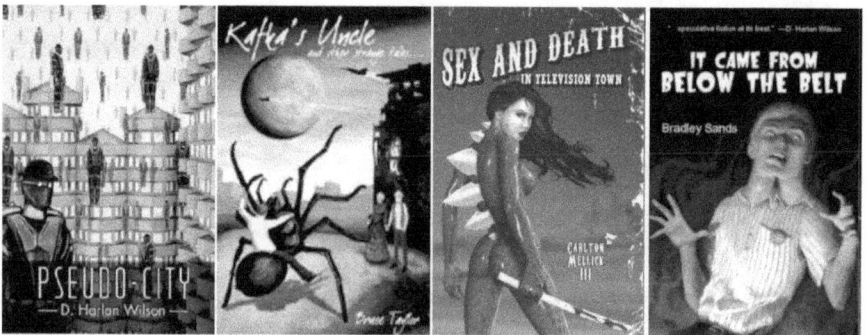

BB-021 "Pseudo-City" D. Harlan Wilson - Pseudo-City exposes what waits in the bathroom stall, under the manhole cover and in the corporate boardroom, all in a way that can only be described as mind-bogglingly irreal. **220 pages $16**

BB-022 "Kafka's Uncle and Other Strange Tales" Bruce Taylor - Anslenot and his giant tarantula (tormentor? fri-end?) wander a desecrated world in this novel and collection of stories from Mr. Magic Realism Himself. **348 pages $17**

BB-023 "Sex and Death In Television Town" Carlton Mellick III - In the old west, a gang of hermaphrodite gunslingers take refuge from a demon plague in Telos: a town where its citizens have televisions instead of heads. **184 pages $12**

BB-024 "It Came From Below The Belt" Bradley Sands - What can Grover Goldstein do when his severed, sentient penis forces him to return to high school and help it win the presidential election? **204 pages $13**

BB-025 "Sick: An Anthology of Illness" John Lawson, editor - These Sick stories are horrendous and hilarious dissections of creative minds on the scalpel's edge. **296 pages $16**

BB-026 "Tempting Disaster" John Lawson, editor - A shocking and alluring anthology from the fringe that examines our culture's obsession with taboos. **260 pages $16**

BB-027 "Siren Promised" Jeremy Robert Johnson & Alan M Clark - Nominated for the Bram Stoker Award. A potent mix of bad drugs, bad dreams, brutal bad guys, and surreal/incredible art by Alan M. Clark. **190 pages $13**

BB-028 "Chemical Gardens" Gina Ranalli - Ro and punk band Green is the Enemy find Kreepkins, a surfer-dude warlock, a vengeful demon, and a Metal Priestess in their way as they try to escape an underground nightmare. **188 pages $13**

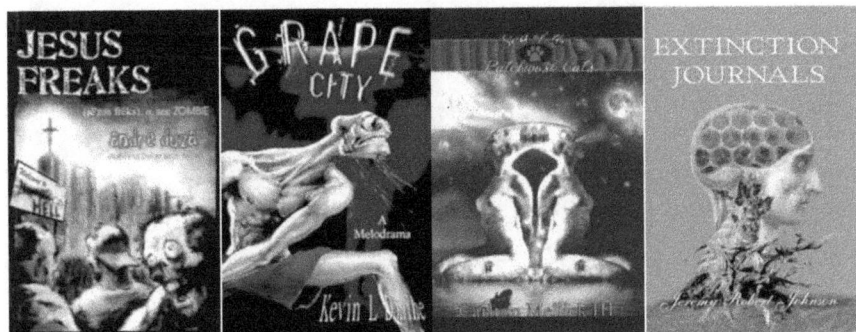

BB-029 "Jesus Freaks" Andre Duza - For God so loved the world that he gave his only two begotten sons… and a few million zombies. **400 pages $16**

BB-030 "Grape City" Kevin L. Donihe - More Donihe-style comedic bizarro about a demon named Charles who is forced to work a minimum wage job on Earth after Hell goes out of business. **108 pages $10**

BB-031"Sea of the Patchwork Cats" Carlton Mellick III - A quiet dreamlike tale set in the ashes of the human race. For Mellick enthusiasts who also adore The Twilight Zone. **112 pages $10**

BB-032 "Extinction Journals" Jeremy Robert Johnson - An uncanny voyage across a newly nuclear America where one man must confront the problems associated with loneliness, insane dieties, radiation, love, and an ever-evolving cockroach suit with a mind of its own. **104 pages $10**

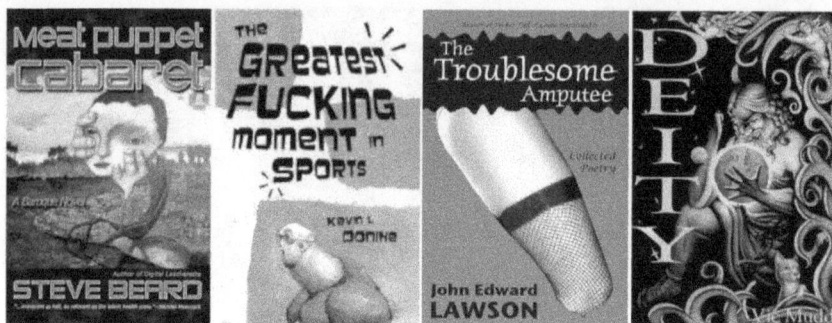

BB-033 "Meat Puppet Cabaret" Steve Beard - At last! The secret connection between Jack the Ripper and Princess Diana's death revealed! **240 pages $16 / $30**

BB-034 "The Greatest Fucking Moment in Sports" Kevin L. Donihe - In the tradition of the surreal anti-sitcom Get A Life comes a tale of triumph and agape love from the master of comedic bizarro. **108 pages $10**

BB-035 "The Troublesome Amputee" John Edward Lawson - Disturbing verse from a man who truly believes nothing is sacred and intends to prove it. **104 pages $9**

BB-036 "Deity" Vic Mudd - God (who doesn't like to be called "God") comes down to a typical, suburban, Ohio family for a little vacation—but it doesn't turn out to be as relaxing as He had hoped it would be... **168 pages $12**

BB-037 "The Haunted Vagina" Carlton Mellick III - It's difficult to love a woman whose vagina is a gateway to the world of the dead. **132 pages $10**

BB-038 "Tales from the Vinegar Wasteland" Ray Fracalossy - Witness: a man is slowly losing his face, a neighbor who periodically screams out for no apparent reason, and a house with a room that doesn't actually exist. **240 pages $14**

BB-039 "Suicide Girls in the Afterlife" Gina Ranalli - After Pogue commits suicide, she unexpectedly finds herself an unwilling "guest" at a hotel in the Afterlife, where she meets a group of bizarre characters, including a goth Satan, a hippie Jesus, and an alien-human hybrid. **100 pages $9**

BB-040 "And Your Point Is?" Steve Aylett - In this follow-up to LINT multiple authors provide critical commentary and essays about Jeff Lint's mind-bending literature. **104 pages $11**

BB-041 "Not Quite One of the Boys" Vincent Sakowski - While drug-dealer Maxi drinks with Dante in purgatory, God and Satan play a little tri-level chess and do a little bargaining over his business partner, Vinnie, who is still left on earth. **220 pages $14**

BB-042 "Teeth and Tongue Landscape" Carlton Mellick III - On a planet made out of meat, a socially-obsessive monophobic man tries to find his place amongst the strange creatures and communities that he comes across. **110 pages $10**

BB-043 "War Slut" Carlton Mellick III - Part "1984," part "Waiting for Godot," and part action horror video game adaptation of John Carpenter's "The Thing." **116 pages $10**

BB-044 "All Encompassing Trip" Nicole Del Sesto - In a world where coffee is no longer available, the only television shows are reality TV re-runs, and the animals are talking back, Nikki, Amber and a singing Coyote in a do-rag are out to restore the light **308 pages $15**

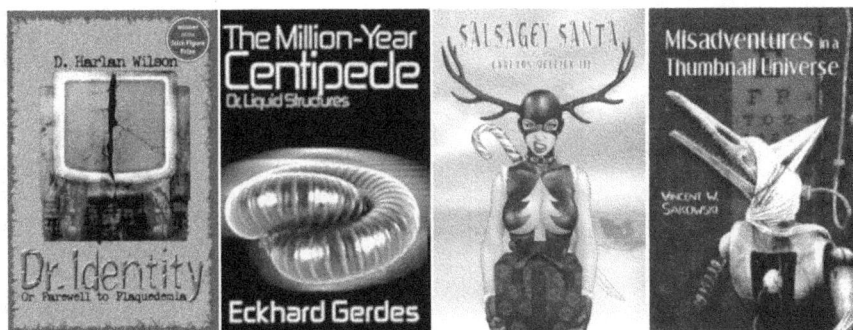

BB-045 "Dr. Identity" D. Harlan Wilson - Follow the Dystopian Duo on a killing spree of epic proportions through the irreal postcapitalist city of Bliptown where time ticks sideways, artificial Bug-Eyed Monsters punish citizens for consumer-capitalist lethargy, and ultraviolence is as essential as a daily multivitamin. **208 pages $15**

BB-046 "The Million-Year Centipede" Eckhard Gerdes - Wakelin, frontman for 'The Hinge,' wrote a poem so prophetic that to ignore it dooms a person to drown in blood. **130 pages $12**

BB-047 "Sausagey Santa" Carlton Mellick III - A bizarro Christmas tale featuring Santa as a piratey mutant with a body made of sausages. 124 pages $10

BB-048 "Misadventures in a Thumbnail Universe" Vincent Sakowski - Dive deep into the surreal and satirical realms of neo-classical Blender Fiction, filled with television shoes and flesh-filled skies. **120 pages $10**

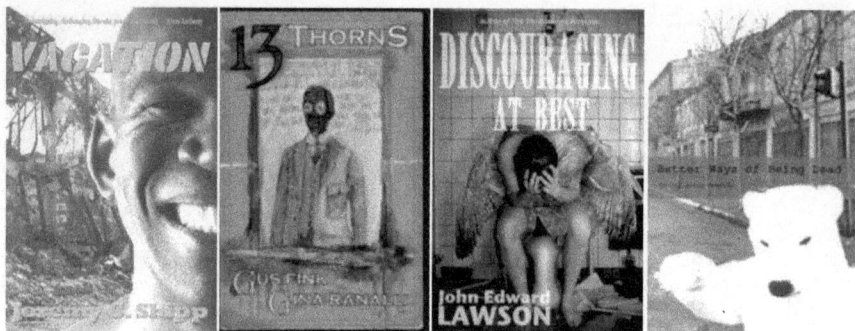

BB-049 **"Vacation" Jeremy C. Shipp** - Blueblood Bernard Johnson leaved his boring life behind to go on The Vacation, a year-long corporate sponsored odyssey. But instead of seeing the world, Bernard is captured by terrorists, becomes a key figure in secret drug wars, and, worse, doesn't once miss his secure American Dream. **160 pages $14**

BB-051 **"13 Thorns"   Gina Ranalli** - Thirteen tales of twisted, bizarro horror. **240 pages $13**

BB-050 **"Discouraging at Best"   John Edward Lawson** - A collection where the absurdity of the mundane expands exponentially creating a tidal wave that sweeps reason away. For those who enjoy satire, bizarro, or a good old-fashioned slap to the senses. **208 pages $15**

BB-052 **"Better Ways of Being Dead"   Christian TeBordo** - In this class, the students have to keep one palm down on the table at all times, and listen to lectures about a panda who speaks Chinese. **216 pages $14**

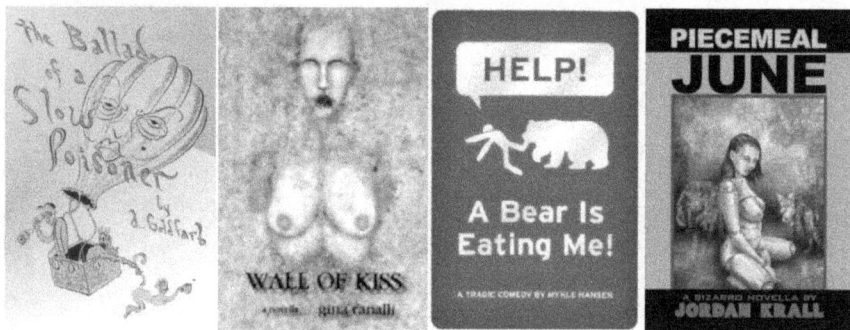

BB-053 **"Ballad of a Slow Poisoner" Andrew Goldfarb** Millford Mutterwurst sat down on a Tuesday to take his afternoon tea, and made the unpleasant discovery that his elbows were becoming flatter. **128 pages $10**

BB-054 **"Wall of Kiss" Gina Ranalli** - A woman... A wall... Sometimes love blooms in the strangest of places. **108 pages $9**

BB-055 **"HELP! A Bear is Eating Me" Mykle Hansen** - The bizarro, heartwarming, magical tale of poor planning, hubris and severe blood loss... **150 pages $11**

BB-056 **"Piecemeal June" Jordan Krall** - A man falls in love with a living sex doll, but with love comes danger when her creator comes after her with crab-squid assassins. **90 pages $9**

BB-057 "Laredo" Tony Rauch - Dreamlike, surreal stories by Tony Rauch. **180 pages $12**

BB-058 "The Overwhelming Urge" Andersen Prunty - A collection of bizarro tales by Andersen Prunty. **150 pages $11**

BB-059 "Adolf in Wonderland" Carlton Mellick III - A dreamlike adventure that takes a young descendant of Adolf Hitler's design and sends him down the rabbit hole into a world of imperfection and disorder. **180 pages $11**

BB-060 "Super Cell Anemia" Duncan B. Barlow - "Unrelentingly bizarre and mysterious, unsettling in all the right ways..." - Brian Evenson. **180 pages $12**

BB-061 "Ultra Fuckers" Carlton Mellick III - Absurdist suburban horror about a couple who enter an upper middle class gated community but can't find their way out. **108 pages $9**

BB-062 "House of Houses" Kevin L. Donihe - An odd man wants to marry his house. Unfortunately, all of the houses in the world collapse at the same time in the Great House Holocaust. Now he must travel to House Heaven to find his departed fiancee. **172 pages $11**

BB-063 "Necro Sex Machine" Andre Duza - The Dead Bitch returns in this follow-up to the bizarro zombie epic Dead Bitch Army. **400 pages $16**

BB-064 "Squid Pulp Blues" Jordan Krall - In these three bizarro-noir novellas, the reader is thrown into a world of murderers, drugs made from squid parts, deformed gun-toting veterans, and a mischievous apocalyptic donkey. **204 pages $12**

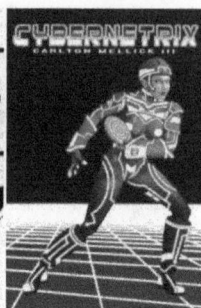

BB-065 "Jack and Mr. Grin" Andersen Prunty - "When Mr. Grin calls you can hear a smile in his voice. Not a warm and friendly smile, but the kind that seizes your spine in fear. You don't need to pay your phone bill to hear it. That smile is in every line of Prunty's prose." - Tom Bradley. **208 pages $12**

BB-066 "Cybernetrix" Carlton Mellick III - What would you do if your normal everyday world was slowly mutating into the video game world from Tron? **212 pages $12**

BB-067 "Lemur" Tom Bradley - Spencer Sproul is a would-be serial-killing bus boy who can't manage to murder, injure, or even scare anybody. However, there are other ways to do damage to far more people and do it legally... **120 pages $12**

BB-068 "Cocoon of Terror" Jason Earls - Decapitated corpses...a sculpture of terror...Zelian's masterpiece, his Cocoon of Terror, will trigger a supernatural disaster for everyone on Earth. **196 pages $14**

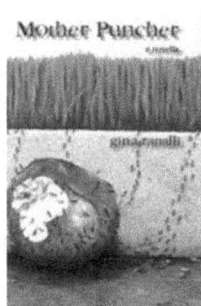

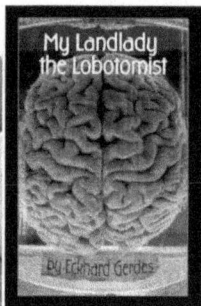

BB-069 "Mother Puncher" Gina Ranalli - The world has become tragically over-populated and now the government strongly opposes procreation. Ed is employed by the government as a mother-puncher. He doesn't relish his job, but he knows it has to be done and he knows he's the best one to do it. **120 pages $9**

BB-070 "My Landlady the Lobotomist" Eckhard Gerdes - The brains of past tenants line the shelves of my boarding house, soaking in a mysterious elixir. One more slip-up and the landlady might just add my frontal lobe to her collection. **116 pages $12**

BB-071 "CPR for Dummies" Mickey Z. - This hilarious freakshow at the world's end is the fragmented, sobering debut novel by acclaimed nonfiction author Mickey Z. **216 pages $14**

BB-072 "Zerostrata" Andersen Prunty - Hansel Nothing lives in a tree house, suffers from memory loss, has a very eccentric family, and falls in love with a woman who runs naked through the woods every night. **144 pages $11**

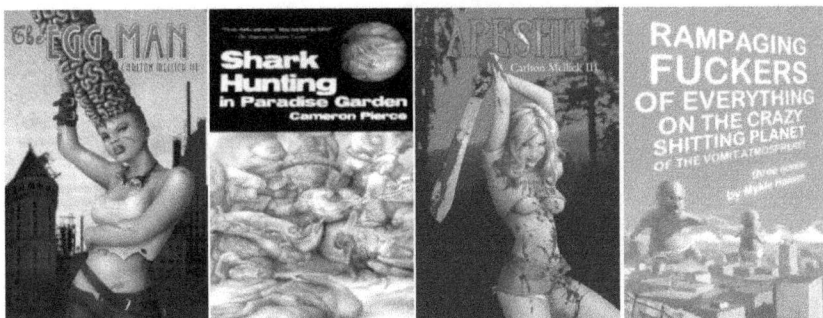

BB-073 "The Egg Man" Carlton Mellick III - It is a world where humans reproduce like insects. Children are the property of corporations, and having an enormous ten-foot brain implanted into your skull is a grotesque sexual fetish. Mellick's industrial urban dystopia is one of his darkest and grittiest to date. **184 pages $11**

BB-074 "Shark Hunting in Paradise Garden" Cameron Pierce - A group of strange humanoid religious fanatics travel back in time to the Garden of Eden to discover it is invested with hundreds of giant flying maneating sharks. **150 pages $10**

BB-075 "Apeshit" Carlton Mellick III - Friday the 13th meets Visitor Q. Six hipster teens go to a cabin in the woods inhabited by a deformed killer. An incredibly fucked-up parody of B-horror movies with a bizarro slant. **192 pages $12**

BB-076 "Rampaging Fuckers of Everything on the Crazy Shitting Planet of the Vomit At smosphere" Mykle Hansen - 3 bizarro satires. Monster Cocks, Journey to the Center of Agnes Cuddlebottom, and Crazy Shitting Planet. **228 pages $12**

BB-077 "The Kissing Bug" Daniel Scott Buck - In the tradition of Roald Dahl, Tim Burton, and Edward Gorey, comes this bizarro anti-war children's story about a bohemian conenose kissing bug who falls in love with a human woman. **116 pages $10**

BB-078 "MachoPoni" Lotus Rose - It's My Little Pony... *Bizarro* style! A long time ago Poniworld was split in two. On one side of the Jagged Line is the Pastel Kingdom, a magical land of music, parties, and positivity. On the other side of the Jagged Line is Dark Kingdom inhabited by an army of undead ponies. **148 pages $11**

BB-079 "The Faggiest Vampire" Carlton Mellick III - A Roald Dahl-esque children's story about two faggy vampires who partake in a mustache competition to find out which one is truly the faggiest. **104 pages $10**

BB-080 "Sky Tongues" Gina Ranalli - The autobiography of Sky Tongues, the biracial hermaphrodite actress with tongues for fingers. Follow her strange life story as she rises from freak to fame. **204 pages $12**

BB-081 "Washer Mouth" Kevin L. Donihe - A washing machine becomes human and pursues his dream of meeting his favorite soap opera star. **244 pages $11**

BB-082 "Shatnerquake" Jeff Burk - All of the characters ever played by William Shatner are suddenly sucked into our world. Their mission: hunt down and destroy the real William Shatner. **100 pages $10**

BB-083 "The Cannibals of Candyland" Carlton Mellick III - There exists a race of cannibals that are made of candy. They live in an underground world made out of candy. One man has dedicated his life to killing them all. **170 pages $11**

BB-084 "Slub Glub in the Weird World of the Weeping Willows"
Andrew Goldfarb - The charming tale of a blue glob named Slub Glub who helps the weeping willows whose tears are flooding the earth. There are also hyenas, ghosts, and a voodoo priest **100 pages $10**

BB-085 "Super Fetus" Adam Pepper - Try to abort this fetus and he'll kick your ass! **104 pages $10**

BB-086 "Fistful of Feet" Jordan Krall - A bizarro tribute to spaghetti westerns, featuring Cthulhu-worshipping Indians, a woman with four feet, a crazed gunman who is obsessed with sucking on candy, Syphilis-ridden mutants, sexually transmitted tattoos, and a house devoted to the freakiest fetishes. **228 pages $12**

BB-087 "Ass Goblins of Auschwitz" Cameron Pierce - It's Monty Python meets Nazi exploitation in a surreal nightmare as can only be imagined by Bizarro author Cameron Pierce. **104 pages $10**

BB-088 "Silent Weapons for Quiet Wars" Cody Goodfellow - "This is high-end psychological surrealist horror meets bottom-feeding low-life crime in a techno-thrilling science fiction world full of Lovecraft and magic..." -John Skipp **212 pages $12**

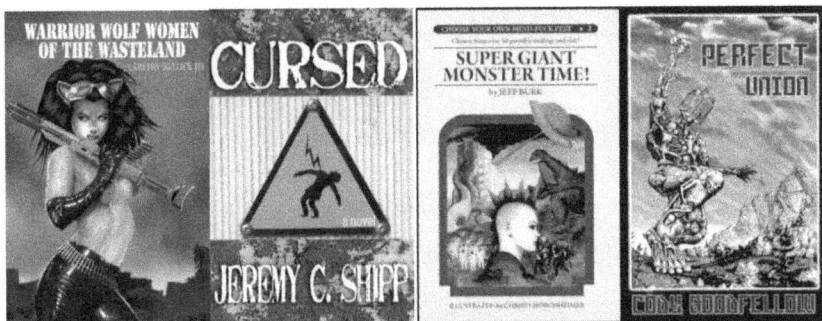

BB-089 "Warrior Wolf Women of the Wasteland" Carlton Mellick III
Road Warrior Werewolves versus McDonaldland Mutants...post-apocalyptic fiction has never been quite like this. **316 pages $13**

BB-090 "Cursed" Jeremy C Shipp - The story of a group of characters who
believe they are cursed and attempt to figure out who cursed them and why. A tale of stylish absurdism and suspenseful horror. **218 pages $15**

BB-091 "Super Giant Monster Time" Jeff Burk - A tribute to choose your
own adventures and Godzilla movies. Will you escape the giant monsters that are rampaging the fuck out of your city and shit? Or will you join the mob of alien-controlled punk rockers causing chaos in the streets? What happens next depends on you. **188 pages $12**

BB-092 "Perfect Union" Cody Goodfellow - "Cronenberg's THE FLY on a
grand scale: human/insect gene-spliced body horror, where the human hive politics are as shocking as the gore." -John Skipp. **272 pages $13**

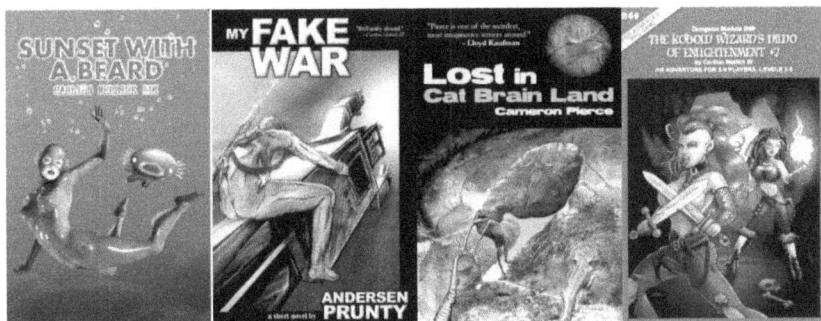

BB-093 "Sunset with a Beard" Carlton Mellick III - 14 stories of surreal
science fiction. **200 pages $12**

BB-094 "My Fake War" Andersen Prunty - The absurd tale of an unlikely soldier
forced to fight a war that, quite possibly, does not exist. It's Rambo meets Waiting for Godot in this subversive satire of American values and the scope of the human imagination. **128 pages $11**

BB-095"Lost in Cat Brain Land" Cameron Pierce - Sad stories from a sur-
real world. A fascist mustache, the ghost of Franz Kafka, a desert inside a dead cat. Primordial entities mourn the death of their child. The desperate serve tea to mysterious creatures. A hopeless romantic falls in love with a pterodactyl. And much more. **152 pages $11**

BB-096 "The Kobold Wizard's Dildo of Enlightenment +2" Carlton
Mellick III - A Dungeons and Dragons parody about a group of people who learn they are only made up characters in an AD&D campaign and must find a way to resist their nerdy teenaged players and retarded dungeon master in order to survive. 232 **pages $12**

COMING SOON

Sinister Miniatures by Kris Saknussemm

Tentacle Death Trip by Jordan Krall

Clockwork Girl by Athena Villaverde

The Tumors Made Me Interesting by Matthew Revert

Homo Bomb by Jeff Burk

ORDER FORM

TITLES	QTY	PRICE	TOTAL

Please make checks and moneyorders payable to ROSE O'KEEFE / BIZARRO BOOKS in U.S. funds only. Please don't send bad checks! Allow 2-6 weeks for delivery. International orders may take longer. If you'd like to pay online via PAYPAL.COM, send payments to publisher@eraserheadpress.com.

SHIPPING: US ORDERS - $2 for the first book, $1 for each additional book. For priority shipping, add an additional $4. INT'L ORDERS - $5 for the first book, $3 for each additional book. Add an additional $5 per book for global priority shipping.

Send payment to:

BIZARRO BOOKS
C/O Rose O'Keefe
205 NE Bryant
Portland, OR 97211

Address	
City	State Zip
Email	Phone